# A HISTORY OF BL

## BLACKFORD
### HISTORICAL SOCIETY

**Series Editor: David Strachan**
Perth and Kinross Heritage Trust

# Contents

Published by Perth and Kinross Heritage Trust 2010
Copyright © Blackford Historical Society

ISBN No. 978-0-9564427-1-0

**Cover Illustration:** *View of Blackford from the Red Brae, May 2005.*
*(© John McLaughlan www.scotlandpics.co.uk)*

# BLACKFORD BEFORE HISTORY

The Blackford area has been home to people for at least 5,000 years. At North Mains, in the northern-most part of the parish, a series of monuments testify to the area's importance in prehistory. A *Neolithic* (c4000-2000 BC) burial mound, and henge monument (a ceremonial site consisting of a circular ditch and earth bank) were excavated in the late 1970s. The henge was found to have contained a timber circle at one point in its use. At both sites, and smaller ones in the immediate area, there was evidence for cremation and burial of the dead ongoing over thousands of years, with different practices reflecting the location's continued importance for the local community through time.

Around the end of the *Neolithic* and the start of the *Bronze Age* (c2000 BC) communities started to erect standing stones and stone circles. There is a standing stone at Peterhead Farm, near to the A9, where Strathallan and Strathearn meet. At Easthill lies the remains of a probable four-poster stone circle, a type of prehistoric monument which is relatively common in Perthshire. Three stones survive but are now divided by the modern Tullibardine road, on the edge of Auchterarder. These monuments would have been used for rituals and ceremonies, perhaps bringing the community together at key times of the year.

*Easthill Stone Circle.*

As the *Bronze Age* (c1500-750 BC) progressed burial practices continued to change, as seen at North Mains. Smaller cairns were constructed to bury the dead, but these were initially for one important person in the community. Cairns with cists (stone lined coffins), have been recorded at Kincardine Glen. It is likely that many more would have existed in the landscape, but have been destroyed by ploughing, as with the remains of cists noted at Barns Farm.

From this period into the Iron Age (c750BC-AD 500) we also have evidence for the buildings which people lived in. Roundhouses (round timber structures with conical roofs) were common through this period and the remains of two have been recorded on the slope to the south-east of East Biggs Farm. Sometimes they are found as individual buildings, but often in groups, as at West Moor and Strathallan Castle. It is likely that many survive undiscovered across the landscape, as shown prior to the recent development of a new golf course to the north of Blackford. There, archaeologists excavated fourteen roundhouses, some in groups, and two within a large palisaded (fenced) enclosure. Often found associated with roundhouses, *souterrains* were underground chambers which are thought to have been used to store foodstuffs. One has been recorded at West Park, with another possible souterrain near Tullibardine Smithy.

*A large palisaded enclosure, containing a roundhouse, excavated in 2007 in advance of the golf course development to the north of Kirkton Farm.*
*(Reproduced courtesy of CFA Archaeology Ltd, Landlines Heritage and Topshot Photography)*

3

*View across part of Blackford Parish to Craig Rossie. (© Perth and Kinross Heritage Trust)*

Around this time ideas appear to have changed, with the construction of the first forts. Whereas in the past archaeologists viewed them as purely defensive, today they are seen as symbols of power, positioned at important and visible locations in the landscape. At Loaninghead, overlooking the modern A9, the fort occupies a prominent position on a natural spur of land, and comprises two ramparts and ditches. The fort at Machany has evidence for vitrification, the melting and fusing of rock and earth through extreme heat, which may reflect a deliberate and dramatic demise for the site. Other forts have been recorded in the parish at Milton of Panholes, North Mains and Waulkmill. Notable hillforts in the wider area include four located around the prominent Craig Rossie in the Ochils, the summit of which dominates the skyline.

Whatever the reason for building the hillforts, their inhabitants would certainly have had to consider their defensive capabilities when the Roman army approached in 80AD to establish the well preserved fort of Ardoch near Braco.

# THE LEGEND OF BLACKFORD

Alongside the sites and settlements which survive in the landscape today, many stories and legends have grown about these remnants of the past.

The most enduring is the legend that the name of the village derives from a tragedy that happened at a ford over the Allan Water. It is believed that a loch used to exist in the area between Blackford and Kinbuck Bridge, stretching for a distance of about fourteen miles and varying from one mile to three miles in width. This loch was said to be a favourite spot of the Caledonian Kings for fishing, and a royal fishing boat was constantly kept at the ready. One of those Kings, reputedly called King Magnus, was accompanied by his Queen (Queen Helen) on a fishing trip to this loch.

The Queen was accidentally drowned at the fordable place on the loch, where a hamlet, now Blackford, stood. Her horse stumbled and threw her into the water where she was swept away by an undercurrent and lost. It is said that the King declared that it was a black ford: the black in this case meaning evil, and so the hamlet by the ford came to be known as the place of the black ford, and to this day is the name of the village.

*The Deaf Knowe.*

After a long search for the body of his Queen, the King decided to have the loch drained for the purpose of recovering the body. After draining the loch and searching for a long time, the remains were at last discovered, but they were in such a state of decomposition they could not be moved, and instead a monumental mound of earth was thrown over the body of Queen Helen. This mound is still in existence today, named "The Deaf Knowe", because a cry from one side goes unheard on the other. The Deaf Knowe is in fact a natural feature, a mound of sand and stone deposited by glacial activity during the last Ice Age.

# EARLY HISTORY

At Peterhead, near to the standing stone and visible from the fort at Loaninghead is a Pictish symbol stone. The stone still retains traces of its symbols; a goose above a rectangle, which would have been much clearer to those viewing the stone after it was carved in the 7th or 8th century AD. Strathallan and Strathearn were part of the Pictish heartlands, and the stone may have been erected to mark a territorial boundary or other important point in the landscape. Recent research has recorded the possible remains of square barrows: Pictish burial mounds, near to the stone, and it is possible that the stone was erected to mark these important burials.

It is likely that some of the fort sites were rebuilt during this period, including the one at Loaninghead, just to the north of the stone. The later first millennium AD also saw the introduction of Christianity, and other important prehistoric sites, such as those at North Mains, were re-used for burial.

# THE MIDDLE AGES

During the medieval period Blackford was located within the Earldom of Strathearn. Earldoms were large territories ruled over by powerful noble families, answerable only to the king. It was at this time that the land was also divided up into parishes.

Small farming communities dotted the landscape governed over by these nobles, and we can see the remnants of this society in the ruins of several medieval castles from Blackford Parish. Kincardine Castle was the principal seat of the Grahams of Montrose, who acquired it during the 1250s. The castle overlooks the Ruthven Water, 5km north-east of Blackford. It was destroyed in 1646 and all that remains today is a ruinous gable wall. Finely sculptured fragments of masonry from the castle have been found, including one piece carved with an image of the classical god Mercury, now held in Perth Museum and Art Gallery.

Gleneagles Castle, located on a prominent knoll at the mouth of Glen Eagles, was a late-medieval towerhouse. The site survives today as a ruin. Two more castles from the area are Ogilvie Castle, a ruinous rectangular tower; and Tullibardine Castle, which does not survive but was once home to William Murray, Marquis of Tullibardine (1689-1746), a prominent Jacobite who participated in both the 1715 and 1746 risings. Murray was eventually captured at Loch Lomond and died in the Tower of London in 1746. The castle was dismantled in 1747 and the last remains swept away c.1830.

*Ruins of Gleneagles Castle. (© Perth and Kinross Heritage Trust)*

*Ruins of Ogilvie Castle.*

The remains of the medieval church can also be found in the parish. Tullibardine Chapel was founded in 1446 by Sir David Murray of Dumbarton. The chapel is largely unaltered from its original plan, with a small tower on the west entered from the church by a narrow doorway. The medieval judges who served the Earls of Strathearn traditionally held lands at Tullibardine.

The settlement of Blackford is first mentioned at this time and is shown on the earliest maps of the area (from the late 16th century) as a small hamlet. Royal control increased in the area during the medieval period with the establishment of Auchterarder as a royal burgh in 1200 AD. This allowed for the levying of tax on traded goods and encouraged the development of the market town. Blackford's location 5km south-west of Auchterarder, on the main Perth to Stirling route, meant it would be closely influenced by the fortunes of the neighbouring burgh during the following centuries.

*The Earls and Dukes of Atholl founded St Mary's Chapel, Tullibardine, in the mid-15th century for family use. (© Perth and Kinross Heritage Trust)*

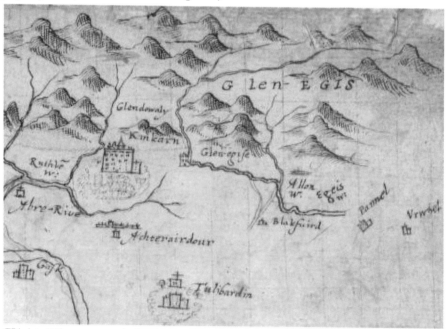

*This late 16th century map by Pont is the earliest known map to show Blackford, then spelt "Blakfuird." (Pont map reproduced by permission of the Trustees of the National Library of Scotland)*

# THE CHURCH

The Parish of Blackford was formerly the Parish of Strageath. The site of Strageath Church was thought to be too remote for the main part of the parish population, and a new church was constructed at Blackford, with its first minister, Alex Gall, inducted in 1574. An Act of Parliament in 1617 officially recognised the relocation of the church from its medieval site at Strageath to Blackford. Now the Old Parish Church, it is located on the hill to the north of the village.

*The Old Parish Church. (© Perth and Kinross Heritage Trust)*

The old cemetery around the ruined Old Parish Church contains several tombstones dating to the 17th century. Of special interest is the Lych Gate, used to rest coffins briefly prior to the burial ceremony commencing within the cemetery. The church was burned in the middle of the 18th century and subsequently rebuilt, but in 1858 it was no longer big enough for the size of congregation, and the present Blackford Parish Church was built in its place, opening in 1859. The bell from the church on the hill is preserved in the present church, and may have come from Strageath, as the inscription on it is pre-Reformation. The Old Parish Church survives as an unroofed ruin, with the bellcote of the church restored in 2007.

*The Lych Gate and one of the many
18th century gravestones in the
Old Parish Church graveyard.
(© Perth and Kinross Heritage Trust)*

The former St Andrew's Free Church was united with the Parish Church in 1950. The St Andrew's Free Church figured prominently in the Disruption in 1843, which started in Auchterarder and quickly spread to Blackford. A number of merchants and villagers met for worship in a stackyard at the west end of the village. In the summer of 1843, after worshipping in the open air without rain for thirteen consecutive Sundays, they concluded that the Lord was with them and they decided to build a church. The foundation stone was laid on the first week in March 1844 and it was completed for Christmas. At the first Communion service held in the Free Church over 100 sat down at the Lord's Table, which included most of the business and professional people of the parish, but the farming community stayed with the Parish Church for fear of the laird terminating their lease.

The St Andrew's Church steeple was struck by lightning in April 1914 and the top half of the steeple demolished. In spite of the Great War it was promptly rebuilt and still stands to this day, although it now houses the local blacksmith's.

The present Parish Church served the community on its own until 1984, when the Rev. James Rennie left. It was subsequently linked with Ardoch and now shares a minister with Ardoch Parish.

*St Andrew's Church was struck by lightning the day before Good Friday 1914. The spire was shattered and the church set on fire. One man was killed and several nearby roofs were damaged by flying masonry. The spire was rebuilt that summer with the repairs being completed shortly after the outbreak of WWI.*

# THE BURNING OF BLACKFORD

After the Battle of Sherrifmuir in November 1715, the Jacobite army burnt the villages of Strathearn as they retreated north towards Perth, an attempt to slow the advance of the government troops. On the 25th January 1716 Blackford was razed. Of all the buildings in the village, only Maitland's Inn and the house of James Davidson, bailiff to the local landowner, survived. It is suggested that they were Jacobite supporters, and smoking stooks (piles of straw) were placed in these buildings in pretence of burning. The rest of the village was destroyed, with its inhabitants left without food or shelter. The leader of the Jacobites, James Stuart, had said that anyone who suffered damage done by the troops should be reimbursed, but it was not until 1722 that the London government arranged for compensation to be paid.

# AGRICULTURE

Agriculture has always figured prominently in the life of Blackford Parish. In the Ochils there is evidence for farming systems dating to before the agricultural improvements. In the summer, livestock was moved from the farms in the lowlands to the upland pasture, a system known as *transhumance*. Shielings, which are small stone and timber huts, were used as accommodation for those tending the herds over the summer months. With changes in the agricultural system, these upland pastures were no longer used, and with it the shielings were abandoned.

In these upland areas there are other remains of pre-improvement farming, such as those at Craigentaggart Hill. The footings of three large rectangular buildings and three small buildings with enclosures have been recorded, arranged around a square courtyard. Around the farm are the remains of rig and furrow cultivation. Across the Ochils there are many other abandoned farms, and the remains of rig and furrow, which can still be seen today.

For many years the parish was part of the Abercairney Estate, belonging to the Morays of Abercairney, who in the first half of the 19th century made the farms into workable units under the 1801 General Enclosure Act. In the case of Blackford the old shielings were amalgamated and enclosed, making farms in the Blackford area mostly around 60 ha (150 acres). The lairds drained the land, in many cases using Irish migrant labour which had built the railway. They built new farmhouses and steadings, which remained as tenanted farms until the latter half of the 20th century.

*Hally's Smiddy, Moray Place.*

*Butter-making classes during WWI.*

*Mill of Ogilvie taken at some point between 1915-20.*

Prior to the early 19th century the crofters mainly grew flax for the weaving industry and barley for the breweries. From the time of the improved farms a large acreage of seed potatoes was grown. Local merchants such as Gilmours sent them south to supply the rich potato growing areas of Eastern England. Livestock started to be kept and several herds of pedigree cattle were set up, two of which, Kincardine Castle and Netherton, are still breeding Aberdeen Angus cattle today.

Well-known studs of Clydesdale horses were founded in the area and one in particular, Bardrill, exported a large number of horses to North America from around 1950 until the 1990s.

In 1952 the Abercairney Estate was bought by Keir & Cawdor, who started to take the tenanted farms into their own hands to farm themselves. In 1975 the Estate was sold to Blackford Farms who continued to farm most of the estate themselves. In 1979 Highland Spring mineral water plant, which is owned by the same owners as Blackford Farms, started to clear all livestock and personnel from any of the farms where they were extracting water. A number of the farms were demolished and no longer exist.

*The introduction of the tractor saw the demise of the horse.*

Today mechanisation has seen a lot more barley grown, and quality livestock is produced on the rich pastures of the Allan valley. Netherton in particular has developed a thriving export trade throughout the world in embryos and semen from their world renowned Aberdeen Angus herd.

# INDUSTRY: BOOTS AND BEER

Traditionally Blackford was a weaving village and flax was grown locally to produce linen. In the near vicinity to the village there is evidence of both a waulkmill and also a dyeworks beside the Buttergask Burn, where it is said cloth came from a wide area to be dyed. The village also contained three tanneries, a gas works and a rope works, though nothing survives on the ground today.

*Moray Street, from the west end looking north, taken in 1899.*

## BOOTMAKING

Prior to the Second World War, Blackford was famous for boots and beer, with the village containing three breweries and two boot factories: most of the boots for the Highland regiments in the First World War were made in Blackford.

The boot-making industry survived for many years in Blackford, with the largest factory surviving until just before the Second World War, producing mainly robust workers' boots. During the War Years troops were billeted at the factory, and at one stage it was used for food storage. In the 1950s it was used as a mushroom factory before finally being demolished in the 1980s to make way for houses.

*Taylor's boot factory, Gleneagles Cottage, Stirling Street, which made soldiers' boots in WWI and Gleneagles shoes, closed in 1937.*

## BREWING

In 1488, King James IV of Scotland, while journeying through Blackford on his way back from his coronation at Scone, is said to have stopped to purchase a barrel of Blackford ale for twelve Scots shillings. This is thought to be the earliest recorded example of a "publick" brewery in Scotland: a brewery brewing commercially for sale.

Although there are no breweries in the village now, in the early 1900s there were three sizeable breweries, and Blackford ale was noted and famed far and wide. The ale was made from the ready supply of fine brewing water from wells within the village, and good quality locally produced malting barley from the Vale of Strathallan.

One of the oldest breweries came into the hands of the Sharp family around 1790 and was developed after 1830 by brothers Robert and Daniel Sharp, building up a reputation around Perth and the East of Scotland for its mild and pale ales. In 1884, R&D Sharp & Co Ltd became the first brewery in Scotland to register as a limited liability public company, with an authorised capital of £25,000. By this time the brothers had died, and the driving force was John Stewart, the former head brewer who became general manager.

The company expanded, purchasing public houses locally and on Tyneside, and rebuilt the brewery to the designs of Russell and Spence, Glasgow architects. A new brewhouse, four storeys high, and maltings were built and fitted with the latest equipment: Morton's horizontal refrigerators; Boby's self-acting screening machines; and Willison's washing machines. The previous brewhouse, which was then used as a store, was thought to date back to 1620.

Alfred Barnard visited the brewery in the 1890s and included it in his book *Noted Breweries of Britain and Ireland*, commenting that there were two wells on the premises which were unusual in that, despite being immediately adjacent to each other, they produced different types of water, being suitable for ale and porter brewing respectively.

Sharp's was the only Blackford brewery to survive the First World War. The 1920s were not good years for the brewing business, however, and when John Stewart died in 1924 the firm lost its impetus, going into liquidation in March 1927. By 1933 the brewery buildings, apart from the offices (now a private house), had been demolished.

William Eadie, who came from a noted family of brewers and maltsters, settled in Blackford in 1809 and established a hotel and livery stables at Moray Street, later adding a small brewhouse. He had fourteen children, with most of his sons entering the brewing trade. One of these, James Eadie, opened the prosperous Cross Street brewery in Burton-on-Trent.

*The cooperage of Sharp's Brewery, Kinpauch Road, which went into liquidation in 1927 with all buildings demolished by 1933.*

In 1896, William Thomson erected a substantial new brewery and malting to the north of Moray Street, beside the now disused Eadie family brewhouse, which was fed by an artesian well. He died during the construction but it continued under the name of W B Thomson Ltd. The company also acquired the Blackford Hotel and added an aerated water factory. It was run by James Thomson Eadie, grandson of William Eadie, who later became a director of William McEwan and Co Ltd, Edinburgh. In March 1915 brewing ceased and the company went into liquidation. The brewery was bought in 1916 by J&A Davidson & Co of Coldstream and then in 1920 by Calders of Alloa. In October 1931, the malting and brewhouse were let on a 21 year lease and later purchased by Gleneagles Maltings Ltd, an associate of Veda Ltd, who marketed Veda Bread, a popular malted wheat product. They were the last commercial traditional floor maltings in Scotland (excluding a number of distilleries who used their floor malting solely for their own purposes). The buildings are now used by Highland Spring.

The third brewery was established by William Eadie's sons, Robert and George, around 1860 and closed around 1910. The building was used for many years as a store by a firm of local potato merchants. In 1947 the buildings were acquired by William Delme-Evans, an engineer, and C I Barrett, a retired excise officer, for Tullibardine Distillery Ltd, and distilling started in 1949. It was later bought by Invergordon distillers. The distillery was purchased by its current owners in 2003 and reopened in 2004, now offering distillery tours.

*Tullibardine Distillery, prior to redevelopment, from the A9.*

# THE ARRIVAL OF THE RAILWAY

The mid-19th century saw a major expansion in railway schemes, and the importance of a railway line from Falkirk to Perth was seen as critical to completing a trunk line from London to the north of Scotland. The Scottish Central Railway Company (SCR) was formed in 1844 and considered two possible routes for the new line. Following a detailed engineering assessment, it was decided that the route through Moncreiffe Hill (to the south of Perth) should be selected, and plans and sections were deposited with the House of Commons for the 1844-45 session.

*Blackford from Kirk Brae around 1910. The large building on the right with the distinctive roof vents is the brewery and maltings erected by W B Thomson Ltd in 1896.*

The plans confirmed that several roads to the north of Blackford would have to be diverted, and that the proposed railway line would separate the village from its church to the north of the main turnpike crossed by the railway. Notably, much of the land in this area was owned by Major William Moray Stirling of Braco, one of the line's promoters.

The Scottish Central Railways Bill eventually received Royal Assent on 1st July 1845 and Major William Moray Stirling was elected as chairman of the newly constituted company. Contracts to construct the line were let in late 1845 and agreement reached on establishing stations at Perth, Forteviot, Dunning, Auchterarder, Blackford, Greenloaning, Dunblane, Bridge of Allan, Stirling and Larbert Junction. By early 1846 most of the land had been acquired, and excavation work involving around 1,800 men and 200 horses was advancing. By early 1847 some 3,886 men and 378 horses were employed and over 2.3 million m³ of earth had been excavated.

It was originally hoped that the line could be opened by spring 1847, but a severe winter delayed progress and the initial opening was rescheduled to early 1848. An unsuccessful request was made to the Board in January 1847 that a bridge should be constructed where the line crossed the turnpike at Blackford, as the road gave access to the church and burial ground and parishioners would be impeded by gates over the railway.

The official opening date was 22nd May 1848 and all passenger arrangements were operating by 1st June, with goods services starting on 15th June. Connecting services to Glasgow and Edinburgh were introduced from 1st July 1848.

The initial scheme was for four trains per day each way and Blackford station, like Forteviot and Dunning, would require one booking clerk, one porter and one point or signalman, along with a policeman or gatekeeper at each level crossing. Blackford station shared the same design as Forgandenny and Kinbuck: a two storey stone building including the station master's accommodation. Each station was later extended, in Blackford's case with a wooden extension.

*Mr Guthrie, Station Master, Blackford Station.*

*James King and fellow Platelayers, Blackford.*

One other notable station was that at Carsebreck, just south of Blackford. This station existed as an intermittent halt; Lord Kinnair of the Dundee & Perth Company had asked the SCR Board in 1851 if land adjacent to the line could be found to create a curling pond. A site was identified at the lochan near Carsebreck House and a plan was submitted in 1852 showing two platforms with a siding and crossover. The halt was at first named the Caledonian Curling Society's Platform; then renamed Curling Pond Halt in 1870; and later referred to as the Royal Curling Club Platform. The first match was played in 1853; one bonspiel was held in the winter of 1882-83; and the final contest was held in 1935 when almost 5,000 players and spectators arrived.

The Scottish Central Railway Company was taken over by the Caledonian Railway Company towards the end of the 19th century. With the steady growth in road network improvements, the general decline in rail services and associated closures began in earnest in the 1930s, with reductions in services progressively taking place up to the 1960s. Sadly, the last passenger train to leave Blackford Station was in June 1956. The resurgence of interest in rail travel in recent years has led to a local campaign that may yet lead to the station re-opening.

# KAY'S AUTOGYRO

An autogiro (or autogyro) is an early type of helicopter. The first experiments with such rotorcraft began in France and Spain, with the first successful flight in 1923 in an aircraft invented by Juan de la Cierva. The term autogiro became a trademark of the Cierva Autogiro Company. Development and progress with such craft was, however, slow, with development halted by the Second World War.

David and Andrew Kay were partners in Kay's Garage, Moray Street, Blackford. David Kay and his friend John Grieve designed their first of three autogiros in the late 1920s. The first machine had a wooden fuselage and an ABC Scorpion engine, and was constructed by Shield's Garage in Perth. It first flew in 1932, but was badly damaged in a heavy landing at Leuchars, Fife, in 1933 and not repaired.

*Kay's Autogyro.*

24

Mr. David Kay, M.B.E.

A second and larger plane was built at Eastleigh, Southampton by Oddie, Bradbury & Cull Ltd. Its maiden flight was described in Flight magazine in December 1934. Although Oddie, Bradbury & Cull Ltd produced two airframes that were delivered to David Kay for finishing, only one was completed. Kay Gyroplanes Limited is known to have presented technical information to Scotland Yard in the late 1930s, following increased interest for the use of autogiros in police aviation. This was not pursued, however, due to the small size of the company, and the aircraft's single seat specification. Unfortunately, insufficient capital resulted in no more experiments and the second machine was taken back to Scotland and put into store in Kay's Garage at Blackford throughout World War II. This machine is now exhibited at the National Museum of Flight at East Fortune, East Lothian. David Kay's call up to the Royal Air Force meant he received little credit for his invention. The patent eventually ran out while he was in the RAF and was subsequently taken up by others.

# BLACKFORD DURING THE WAR YEARS

Like most villages Blackford was greatly affected by both World Wars, losing 26 men in the 1914-18 conflict, and twelve in the 1939-45 war. They are commemorated on the War Memorial at the west end of the village.

During the First World War the boot factories were working flat out manufacturing boots for the Scottish regiments, and for a time soldiers were camped on the White Muir during training exercises.

In 1940 the remnants of the Tank Corps, which escaped from Dunkirk, took over Carsebreck Station and also commandeered the steading at Netherton and three rooms of the farmhouse for an officers' mess. They remained there for the summer of 1940 and while there were re-equipped with around 20 new tanks. In the late autumn of that year they moved to Blackford, commandeering the boot factory and maltings for billeting the soldiers, and Blackford Lodge as an officers' mess. The tanks were lined along Stirling Street and went for daily training up on the Sheriffmuir. Up until the spring of 1944 Blackford remained a garrison town with several different regiments

*Blackford carters with Black Watch Territorials at the Volunteers Training Camp at White Muir in 1914. The carts carried provisions from the railway station to the camp.*

*Children collecting for wounded during WWI at Games Park.*

of Tank Corps and Artillery stationed in the village. In the final year of the war the boot factory and maltings were used for storing food, including animal feed.

Agriculture played a big part in the war effort and acres of land which had not been ploughed before were brought into production and compulsorily made to grow grain, potatoes and flax. Farm labour was scarce because so many men were serving in the armed forces, but soldiers were made available to help during busy periods and towards the end of the war Italian and German prisoners of war were sent out to work on the farms. To help with the war effort schools were given three weeks holiday in October so that children could help to pick potatoes.

In 1940, eighteen school children from Glasgow were evacuated to Blackford and later the same year this number rose to 30. Many of that first group did not stay as they could not cope with country life. A second group of 36 arrived in March 1941 after the Clydebank blitz, with most staying until 1944-45. Between April and July 1941 there were approximately 75 evacuees living in Blackford and the surrounding area. During the peak period the school could not cope with the increased numbers, and for a time local children went to school in the forenoon and the evacuees in the afternoon. After a time a fourth classroom was brought into use with another teacher so that all children could have a full day's education. In July 1941 around 25 to 30 of the evacuees returned to Glasgow, though most of the remainder stayed until nearer the end of the war.

# SPORTS AND PASTIMES

For a small village, Blackford residents engaged in a wide range of activities. The famous Blackford Highland Games started in 1869, and while originally run in August, as a result of many wet years they are now held on the last Saturday in May. They moved from a site near the railway station, Station Park, to their current site at the Games Park prior to the First World War.

*Games Park in the 1940s, before the small hall was built.*

The Golf Club, with a 9-hole golf course, was situated behind the Old Manse (now known as Brookfield). When the Queen's Course at Gleneagles was built, around 1930, the land at Blackford was incorporated into it and members were offered life membership of Gleneagles Golf Course.

The Bowling Club has been in existence since 1859 and was originally on ground at the side of Bank House on Moray Street. The present bowling club is situated on part of the games field and was opened by Miss Richardson of Dunblane in 1924.

*Blackford Bowling Club.*

*Grand Match at Carsebreck in 1898. (Reproduced courtesy of the Royal Caledonian Curling Club)*

Outdoor curling was held at Carsebreck, near the railway line, midway between Greenloaning and Blackford stations. The landowners gave the necessary access from the railway and use of the land for the Grand Match or Bonspiel. This was a traditional match between North and South Scotland, which took place when weather conditions were suitably frosty. In total 25 matches were held between 1853 and 1935. With the nationalisation of the railways in the mid-20th century, access to the site changed and the co-ordinating Royal Caledonian Curling Association decided in 1947 to dismantle their boardroom and relocate the Grand Match to the Lake of Menteith.

As well as the Carsebreck club, Blackford also had a local curling club at this time, playing at White Muir, located between Blackford and Gleneagles. In 1949 the two clubs amalgamated and it became known as the Blackford and Carsebreck Curling Club, which still exists today.

The village had a large number of clubs and groups, including: Blackford Cycling Club (1909); Allan Vale Football Club (1920s); a Drama Club (1960s); and a Rifle Club (1910s). The Scottish Women's Rural Institute started in 1934 and is still going strong. A Flower Show was in existence in 1895, the same year as the lemonade factory was established, and is still running today. There was also a cricket club in the early 1900s, consisting mainly of local farmers, whom the Blackford Estate shooting tenant persuaded to form a team to play games against his guests.

# HIGHLAND SPRING

Water has always been of central importance to Blackford. In the 1970s the decision was made to set up Highland Spring to bottle and sell water worldwide. Before Blackford was chosen as the source of supply, other sites in Wales and in the Highlands were considered, but Blackford was selected as its water supply was readily available, plentiful, pure, clean and easily accessible for road and rail links. Scotland's image of unspoiled natural beauty and the association of pure spring water also played a major factor in bringing the business to Blackford in 1979.

Highland Spring is now the leading UK-produced brand of bottled water and its land is certified organic by the Soil Association. The plant has a catchment area in the Ochil Hills of 1,000 hectares, with the water taking fifteen years to filter through the basalt and sandstone strata to boreholes lined with stainless steel, which allow the water to be gently pumped to the surface and then down to the bottling plant.

The Blackford headquarters boasts one of Europe's most modern plants, with four state-of-the-art bottling lines, producing one million bottles a day.

*The countryside surrounding Blackford looking north from the Ochils. (Reproduced courtesy of Highland Spring)*

# MODERN BLACKFORD

The layout of the present day village has arisen historically from the original street pattern based around Stirling Street. It was the main road up until the mid-1800s when the advent of toll roads funded a new main thoroughfare, Moray Street. The dwellings in Stirling Street were feud out in 1796 and were largely owned by their occupants. Following the setting out of Moray Street new houses and shops were built, many of which were rented out to the inhabitants, giving rise to the notion that Stirling Street was the more wealthy part of the village, as houses were mainly owned rather than rented.

In the early days of the 20th century many shops and other businesses existed in the village. By the beginning of the 1970s there were only seven shops in Moray Street, with most of the others converted into houses. The Post Office (now Blackford Village Store) and the 'Roll on In' (formerly the butcher's shop) still exist today, as does the Blackford Hotel, along with a new retail complex, Eaglesgate, which has been constructed at the south-west entrance to the village. Several shops and two restaurants are already open and it is hoped more will follow in the near future. Other businesses still in existence in the village include the Blackford Inn, McNaughton's Garage and D&M Woods, the local blacksmiths.

Three large stone villas were built at the west end of the village around 1900, and two bungalows adjacent to them around 1930, but the village remained static until the middle of the 20th century when a council housing scheme was started by Perthshire County Council, at the east end of the village in Abercairney Place. This was augmented gradually and extended to include housing in Moray Place and Arnott Road. A small development of council houses at Ogilvie Place, at the west end of the village, was also built. Many of these houses have been sold under the right to buy legislation.

The first major development, since the council housing at Ogilvie Place, was erected, from 2004 onwards, at Abercairney Close. There, Hillcrest Housing Association developed a small social housing scheme of 14 houses, in partnership with the developers for the Mill of Ogilvie site where 50 private houses have been built to date. Plans are pending to build a further 180 or so houses, divided between affordable dwellings at Abercairney, and more private housing at the Old Mill site. The present number of houses in the village is around 330 and the proposed dwellings will increase this to just over 500.

In addition to the housing within the village boundary there are plans to build shared ownership and luxury housing at the new GWest golf development to the north east. The golf course is now almost complete and building is expected to begin on the housing in the near future.

It is curiously apt that the most recent residential development in the area resulted in the discovery of the earliest known - the Bronze and Iron Age houses uncovered between 2006 and 2008. They are also a reminder of the rich and varied archaeological heritage of Blackford Parish, with sites reflecting its important role in medieval Scotland. The more recent history of Blackford village itself has in many ways been tied to water and from ale to whisky and now back to water; it is certainly part of its future. In the modern age, attached to the major thoroughfare of the A9, Blackford looks set to continue to thrive as a growing community with a long and fascinating past.

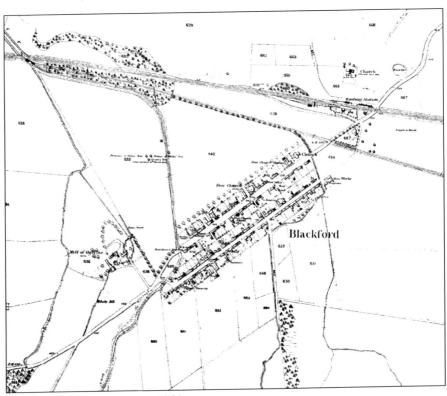

*Ordnance Survey 1st edition map c1866.*
*(Reproduced by permission of Ordnance Survey on behalf of HMSO. Ordnance Survey Licence number 100016971 (2010))*